THE PUPPY PLACE

GOL...

ELLEN
MILES

A
LITTLE APPLE
PAPERBACK

SCHOLASTIC INC.

New York   London   Toronto   Auckland   Sydney
Mexico City   Hong Kong   New Delhi   Buenos Aires

For the original Sammy, my best reading friend

ISBN-13: 978-0-439-79379-7
ISBN-10: 0-439-79379-3

25 24 23 22 21 20 19   9 10 11 12/0

Printed in the U.S.A.   40

First printing, September 2005

CHAPTER ONE

Charles woke up with a bad feeling in his stomach. Why? For a minute, he couldn't figure it out. Then he rolled over and looked at his clock. It was 3:46 A.M., and Charles could hear the loud "deedle-deedle-dee" of his dad's pager going off. Mr. Peterson was a fireman. When his pager went off, there was a fire somewhere in town.

Charles listened to his dad's footsteps going downstairs. Then he heard the slam of a truck door and an engine starting up. He lay there for a while, worrying a little. He decided to stay awake until his dad came home.

But he must have fallen asleep, because when he woke up again, the sun was shining and his clock said it was 7:16. Charles rubbed his eyes and climbed out of bed. Then he raced down to the kitchen and looked out the window.

Dad's red pickup was not in the driveway.

Mom was making French toast while the Bean—Charles's little brother—crawled around on the floor by her feet. The smell of cinnamon made Charles's mouth water. "Is Dad —" Charles began.

"Dad's fine," Mom said. "He called a little while ago. There was a big fire, but everyone is okay."

Charles let out a big breath. It was cool to have a fireman dad, but scary sometimes, too.

"He'll be home soon," Mom told Charles.

"Where was the fire?" asked Lizzie, scuffing her slippers as she shuffled into the kitchen. She rubbed her eyes and yawned. Lizzie was Charles's older sister. It always took her a long time to wake up.

"Out at a farm in Middletown," Mom said.

At this, Lizzie's eyes popped open. "Were any animals hurt?" she asked.

Mom shook her head. "I don't think so." She flipped a slice of French toast. "Set the table, okay?" Mom asked.

That *proved* that everything was okay. What could be more normal than doing chores?

Since there was no reason to worry, Charles decided to ask his favorite question, the one he asked every single morning.

"So *why* can't we have a dog?" he asked.

His mother sighed. "Again?" She pulled the orange juice out of the fridge and filled four glasses and the Bean's purple sippy cup. "Do we have to talk about this every day?"

"Only until we get a dog," Lizzie said, with a sleepy smile.

"First you said we couldn't have a dog because our apartment was too small," Charles reminded his mom. "Then we moved to this big old house, and now there is plenty of room." He followed Lizzie around the table, putting a fork onto every napkin she laid down. "But instead of adopting a dog, we adopted the Bean. "

Charles looked down at the Bean. Sometimes Charles could hardly remember the Bean's real name. It was Adam. But they had called him the Bean ever since he came to live with them when he was a tiny squirmy baby. "Just a little bean," Mr. Peterson had said, and the name had stuck.

The Bean grinned up at Charles and made a little woofing noise. "Even though he *thinks* he's a dog, he's *not*," Charles pointed out. "He's just a kid who likes to crawl around on the floor, beg for food, and sleep on a fleece dog bed."

"And carry his stuffed toys in his mouth," Lizzie added.

"It's a phase," their mom said, the way she always did. "He'll get over it by the time he's —"

"Seventeen," Charles finished, the way their

dad always did. It was their dad's favorite joke. Their mom didn't think it was so funny.

"Anyway," Charles continued, "back then you said a baby and a dog were too much at once. You said we had to wait until the Bean was older. Well, now he *is*. He's not a baby anymore."

"No, he's not," agreed his mother, a little sadly. She loved babies. And kittens. Just not puppies. Mr. Peterson always joked about his wife being a cat person, not a dog person. Mrs. Peterson always said she didn't see anything wrong with that. She had grown up with cats and she was used to cats. But the other family members were not interested in cats. The rest of the family loved dogs.

"So, why can't we get a puppy?" Charles and Lizzie asked together.

"Jinx," Charles said to Lizzie. "Owe me a favor. You clear the table after we eat."

Lizzie stuck out her tongue. Charles grinned. He *always* said "jinx" first.

"We *will* have a puppy," their mother said. "Someday. When the time is right, and the puppy is right."

"But when will that be?" Charles asked. "When *I'm* seventeen?" Sometimes he felt as if he'd waited *forever* for a dog. It wasn't fair. Everybody *else* had dogs. And nobody wanted one more than Charles and Lizzie and the Bean. Nobody would take better care of a dog, or teach it as many great tricks, or love it as much as they would.

"We'll know," Mom said. "When the time is right, we'll know." She had that tone in her voice, the tone that meant it was time to change the subject.

But Lizzie didn't seem to notice. "If we had a dog, we'd all feel better," she said. "Did you know that dog owners are happier, healthier, and more relaxed than people who don't have dogs? Plus, having a dog teaches kids responsibility. And a dog can help to protect the house and save people from fires."

Mom held up both hands. "Enough!" she cried. "I've heard all your facts before, Lizzie, and I know they're all true. I also know that puppies are a lot of work and cause a lot of mess and trouble." She turned back to the skillet on the stove.

Charles knew what she was thinking. Dogs shed fur all over the place. They chew things. They knock over garbage cans. They bark. There were lots of reasons for not getting a dog. Mom didn't even have to spell it out anymore.

This time, even Lizzie seemed to understand that the subject was closed. She slid into her seat and picked up the newspaper. "Cool, Mom," she said. "Your story about the school board meeting is on the front page."

"I bet Mr. Baker will ask me to write about this fire, wherever it was," Mom said. Mr. Baker was the editor of the *Littleton News*, and Mrs. Peterson's boss. She wiped her hands on a towel. "I'll give him a call as soon as your dad gets home." She looked at the clock. "I'm surprised Dad's not here already. I guess we'd better start breakfast without him, or you two will be late for school."

"I hope he gets here before we have to go," said Charles.

Mom piled two plates with French toast and brought them to the table. Then she cut up another piece and put the Bean's plate on the floor next to Charles's feet. Charles had noticed that she had given up on trying to make the Bean sit in his high chair. "Maple syrup?" she asked, passing the bottle to Charles.

Charles poured a big glug of syrup onto his toast. Then he remembered his new joke. Charles told a joke almost every morning. "Hey! Knock, knock," he said.

"Watch the syrup," said Mom.

"You're supposed to say, 'Who's there?'" he reminded her. Then he looked down at his plate. "Oops." The syrup had practically drowned his French toast.

Mom sighed and held out her hand for the bottle. "Who's there?" she asked.

"The interrupting cow," Charles said.

"The interr—" Mom began. But before she could finish, Charles jumped in.

"Moo." He cracked up. "Get it?" he asked. "The interrupting cow?"

Charles had only taken one bite of his breakfast when he heard his dad's pickup pull into the driveway. A minute later, Dad trudged into the kitchen. His shoulders were slumped, his face was smudged with soot, and his hair was all flattened from being under his helmet.

"Dad!" cried Lizzie, jumping up to hug him.

"Hey, punkin," he said tiredly.

Charles noticed a big bulge underneath his dad's jacket. "What's that?" he asked, pointing.

Then he noticed that the bulge was moving.

Charles came closer. The bulge was squiggling and squirming all over the place.

9

Dad smiled and pulled the zipper of his coat down a few inches.

"Meet Goldie," he said. Charles saw two chocolate-brown eyes, a pair of floppy ears, a twitching black nose, and a furry, golden face all streaked with soot.

"A puppy!" Charles yelled.

CHAPTER TWO

"What?" Mom stared at Dad.

He didn't look back at her. "Yup," he said to Charles. "It's a puppy. A golden retriever. She's only about ten weeks old. I don't think she's hurt, but she's a pretty scared little girl."

The puppy peeked out at this new place. She wanted to explore and run and sniff and taste. But first — was it safe? She had to know.

Carefully, Charles moved closer. Very slowly, he put his hand up near the puppy's nose so she could sniff him. "She's beautiful," he whispered.

"Doggy!" yelled the Bean.

The puppy flinched at the loud noise. "It's okay," Charles told her softly. "You're safe."

"Paul —" Mom began. Charles could tell by his

mom's voice that his dad had not told her about the puppy.

"I know, Betsy," Dad said, holding up his hand. "I should have asked first. But she's such a little thing, and she's been through so much." He pulled out a chair and sat down. The puppy peered from his jacket with big, frightened eyes.

Lizzie was staring at the little dog. "She is the cutest thing I ever *saw*," she said finally. "We're keeping her, right?"

The grown-ups looked at each other.

"Look," said Dad. "This little pup is going to need a home. The people who owned the house and barn that just burned down aren't going to be able to keep Goldie. They asked me to take her — just until we can find her a good home."

"A foster puppy!" Lizzie said. Before they had adopted the Bean, the Petersons had taken care of a couple of foster children, kids who had needed a safe, temporary home.

"We'll take care of her," Charles said. "We'll

12

feed her and walk her and brush her and teach her manners and show her tricks and clean up when she makes mistakes and —"

"Charles," Mom said.

"We'll make sure she's happy and safe forever and ever," Charles finished.

"Charles," Mom said again. "Hold on there, bucko." She folded her arms against her chest and leaned against the refrigerator.

Charles couldn't stand it. "Please?" he begged. "Please?"

"Your father and I will need to talk this over," Mom said. "It's a big decision."

Just then, the back door swung open and Sammy strolled in. "Knock, knock," he said.

"Who's there?" Charles asked automatically.

"Kayak," said Sammy as he picked up a plate and helped himself to the last piece of French toast in the skillet. Charles's best friend came next door for a second breakfast at the Petersons' nearly every morning.

"Kayak who?" Charles asked.

"Kayak you a question?" Sammy said. Both boys cracked up.

Mom rolled her eyes. "Have some breakfast, Sammy," she said.

"Thanks!" Sammy said cheerfully. He pulled out the chair next to Charles's, sat down, and reached for the syrup. Then he glanced at Mr. Peterson and almost dropped the syrup bottle. "Whoa!" he said. "A puppy!"

"Her name is Goldie," Charles reported. "We might get to keep her."

"I bet Rufus looked just like that when he was a puppy," Sammy said. "'Course, that was before I was born, so I don't remember." Sammy's dog was a golden retriever, too. Rufus had been around as long as Charles could remember. He was a big, strong dog with a beautiful reddish-gold coat and a sweet face.

"Golden retrievers are one of the most popular breeds in America," Lizzie said. "They're also one of the most intelligent, loyal, and athletic." She was quoting from her "Dog Breeds of the World" poster. Lizzie knew every fact about every dog, from Airedales to Yorkies.

"Rufus isn't so athletic anymore," Sammy said. "He just lies there looking sad most of the time. He used to like to run and play ball. Now he's boring."

"Dogs slow down when they get older," Charles's dad said.

"Rufus isn't *that* old." Sammy poured some more syrup on his plate.

"Maybe he's bored," Lizzie said. "Have you tried getting him some new toys?"

Sammy nodded. "I saved my allowance for two whole weeks so I could buy him this cool flying saucer. He barely even looked at it."

"Maybe he's tired," Lizzie suggested. "Maybe he needs some doggy vitamins."

Sammy shook his head. "We tried that. I even tried putting coffee in his water bowl. Nothing perks him up. Right, Charles?"

"What?" Charles wasn't listening. He was just looking at Goldie. And she was looking back at him. He reached out again and gently scratched her between her soft little ears.

The puppy liked that.

She decided that this new place was a good place. A safe place.

It was time to explore.

CHAPTER THREE

Goldie started to wriggle, pushing her way out of Dad's jacket. She got one paw out and started to push harder. Her little legs churned away as she climbed.

"Oops! Hold on there, sweetie," Charles's dad said. He pulled down the zipper and reached in with a big hand to carefully pull her out. "There you go," he said as he bent down to put Goldie on the floor.

The puppy looked around with big eyes. She yawned widely, showing a long, curled pink tongue and two rows of tiny, sharp white teeth. Then she shook herself and took a couple of unsteady steps. Her little tail stuck straight up in the air. Her golden coat was tangled and smudged with soot.

"Doggy!" yelled the Bean. He started to crawl toward Goldie.

Mom swooped down to pick the Bean up. "Let's let the doggy get used to us slowly," she said. She kissed the Bean's ear and held him tight. He yawned, showing off his own pink tongue and little white teeth.

Goldie took three steps forward, then stopped, trembling. This room was warm and it smelled good, but it was big, and there were so many people in it!

Charles sat down on the floor and reached out a hand. "Here, Goldie," he called. Goldie padded toward him.

"She knows her name!" Lizzie cried softly. "What a little smartie!" She sat down on the floor next to Charles. "Are you sure she's not hurt, Dad?" she asked. "Did you check her all over?"

"Not yet," said Dad. "We can clean her up and make sure she's okay. She's had all her puppy shots, so unless she's hurt, we don't need to take her to the vet."

Sammy finished his French toast and stood up. "I'll go get some of Rufus's old toys," he said. "Goldie might as well borrow them if he's not using them."

He headed for the door.

"Plate, Sammy," Mrs. Peterson reminded him.

Sammy went back to the table, grabbed his plate and fork, and brought them to the sink. "I'll be right back, Goldie," he promised as he let himself out.

Dad took a clean towel out of a drawer, wet a corner of it at the sink, and joined Charles and Lizzie on the floor. "Let's take a look at this pup," he said.

But when Dad reached for Goldie, she scooched down, her eyes wide and her ears held back. She tucked herself under Charles's knee.

"She's still scared," said Charles. "It's okay,

girl," he said softly. "Come on, Goldie. I'll hold you so Dad can check you out." He held out his hands and Goldie climbed into his lap, making little snuffling noises as she curled into his arms.

Charles leaned down and buried his nose in the silky-soft fur of Goldie's neck. He took a big, deep breath. Ahh! That delicious puppy smell! Charles felt perfectly happy, sitting there on the floor with a warm dog on his lap.

With Charles holding her to keep her calm, Lizzie and her dad wiped Goldie's coat clean and checked her all over to make sure she had no cuts or bruises. By the time they were done, Goldie wasn't frightened anymore. She started to mouth their hands as they petted her, gnawing with her little teeth.

"Hey!" cried Charles. "Do I look like a puppy to you?" He knew that puppies chewed on one another all the time. Goldie would have to learn that chewing on people was not okay.

Charles held Goldie in his arms, giggling as she

licked and chewed at his earlobes. Then she strug-gled to get down, and he let her go. She skidded across the kitchen floor, heading straight for the Bean's plate of French toast.

"Hold on!" said Charles. "That's not puppy food!" He scrambled to get to the plate before Goldie did.

Goldie sat back, looking disappointed. Then she caught another smell and took off in the other direction, tripping over herself in her eagerness to learn everything about this new place.

Sammy burst back in with an armload of fuzzy, floppy toys. "I brought Mr. Man and Yellow Duckie," he said. "Duckie used to be Rufus's favorite."

The Bean held out his hands. "Toy!" he yelled.

Sammy handed him Mr. Man, who was made out of a soft white material. Then he held out Duckie for Goldie. She took hold of one of the floppy yellow wings and started to shake the toy wildly, making the other wing bang against her head. Losing her balance, she plopped down on the floor and rolled over so her soft, pink belly showed.

Her eyes were wild as she bit at the toy, grabbing for Duckie's beak. Duckie suddenly let out a loud squeak. Goldie jumped up and stared at the toy for a second. Then she grabbed a wing and started shaking again.

Everybody was laughing. Goldie was so funny! Charles thought he could watch her forever.

"Oh, Mom," said Lizzie. "We *have* to keep her."

"Please?" Charles begged.

"If we keep her, it will only be for a little while," Mrs. Peterson reminded them. "Just until we find her a good home. That's how a foster family works."

"We'll take good care of her," Charles promised. "She won't be any trouble!"

Just then, Goldie rolled over, jumped to her feet, and took three steps to a spot under the kitchen table.

She sniffed.

She squatted.

And she peed.

CHAPTER FOUR

"It was only a little puddle," Sammy said. "I don't know why your mom got so upset." He kicked a stone between the two big maple trees at the end of the Dodsons' driveway. "Goal!"

Charles, Lizzie, and Sammy were walking to school together, the way they always did. Charles and Sammy were both in Mr. Mason's second-grade class. Lizzie was in fourth. It had not been easy to say good-bye to Goldie. Charles could still practically see her big eyes watching him curiously as he helped Lizzie clean up the puppy's "mistake."

Would she still be there when he got home from school? *We have to convince Mom to let us be her foster family*, he thought. His fists were all balled up inside his jacket pockets. He almost felt like he might cry. He took a deep breath. "We have to make a plan," he said. "First we convince Mom to let us foster Goldie. Then we convince her to let us keep her forever."

Lizzie grinned at him. "I'm with you," she said.

Sammy bumped fists with Charles. "Me, too."

Charles had a hard time paying attention in school that day. And it wasn't because he was making up new knock-knock jokes. It was because he could not stop thinking about Goldie. What was she doing? Was she still feeling scared? Was Mom making sure that she had enough clean, fresh water? Was she making sure that the Bean was not bothering Goldie?

Mr. Mason called on Charles three times during math, even though Charles did not raise his hand. Subtraction was not usually hard for Charles, but today it was.

First Mr. Mason wanted to know how many cherries Anna would have left if she started with thirteen and gave Charles eight. "Seven?" Charles guessed. He knew it was wrong as soon as he said it.

Mr. Mason just shook his head and moved on. Later, he tried Charles again. "What if I had eleven elephants," he asked, "and I gave you three?"

Charles pictured three huge elephants squeezed trunk-to-tail into his living room. Then he pictured a tiny but ferocious Goldie running around their huge feet, barking at them. He smiled.

"Charles?" Mr. Mason was waiting.

"Um," said Charles. "Seven?" Again, he knew it was wrong.

The third time, Charles didn't even hear Mr. Mason call on him. Sammy finally poked Charles in the side. "Wake up," said Sammy.

Charles didn't know what the question was. "Seven?" he guessed.

"Correct!" said Mr. Mason, with a big smile. "Now you're getting it."

The only time Charles really paid attention was

during Reading Partners time, when his class went down the hall to read with their kindergarten friends. Charles had a partner named Oliver, a funny little boy who wore big glasses. Oliver always wanted to read about dogs. That day, he showed Charles a book called *Why Do Dogs Bark?* that was full of interesting facts about dogs. Charles was happy to read that book with Oliver. It made him think of Goldie.

Finally, finally, school was over. It was time to go home and see Goldie again! Charles could have run the whole way home, but Lizzie and Sammy were walking along slowly, talking about how to convince Mom to let them keep Goldie.

"I spent my whole turn on the computer looking up how to housebreak puppies," Lizzie reported. Fourth graders got a half hour of computer time every day. She showed them a bunch of articles she had printed out. "Goldie's so smart. She'll learn to go to the bathroom outside in no time."

"I had this great idea," Sammy said. "We just

need a little tiny tape recorder that we can hide under your parents' bed."

Charles stared at his friend. "What?" Sammy was always coming up with the wildest ideas.

"It's easy," said Sammy. "We just make this tape that says, 'You want a dog. You love dogs. You love Goldie. You want to keep her.'" He was talking like a robot. "Then we leave it under your mom's bed so it plays at night while she's sleeping," he explained in his normal voice. "So she gets kind of, you know, hypnotized."

Lizzie laughed. "You want to hypnotize my mom?"

"Right," said Sammy. "Believe me, it'll work. I saw this guy at the fair last year? He convinced a lady that she was a chicken. She was squawking and flapping her wings, and —"

Charles had tuned out. He was thinking about Goldie again. He could hardly wait to pick her up and hold her in his arms.

Sammy went home to check on Rufus, and

Charles and Lizzie went up their walk. Mom opened the door when she heard them on the front porch steps. She looked very tired. Her hair was all straggly. The Bean was on the floor by her right foot, and Goldie was by her left foot.

"Uff!" barked Goldie. She looked happy to see Charles and Lizzie.

"Uff!" barked the Bean. He looked happy, too.

Mom was holding something in her hand. It was one of her running shoes — or at least something that *used* to be a shoe.

"Mom," said Lizzie, holding up her articles. "I bet I can housebreak Goldie in one week!"

"And I'll make a bed for Goldie in my room," Charles said, "so I can watch her at night, and —"

Mom held up her hand, the one that wasn't clutching the chewed-up sneaker. "Don't even bother trying to convince me," she said. "I've already made up my mind."

CHAPTER FIVE

"But Mom —!" Charles said.

"I knew it!" Lizzie wailed. "I just knew you wouldn't let us keep her."

Mom looked from Charles to Lizzie and back to Charles again. "Don't you want to wait and hear what I decided before you get all upset?" she asked. "Come on, let's go have a snack and talk about it." She led them to the kitchen. Goldie trotted ahead of her, slipping and sliding a little on the wood floor. The Bean ran along on his short little legs, yelling, "Dodie, Dodie!"

"Dodie?" Lizzie asked. This was a new word for the Bean.

"It's how he says Goldie," her mom explained, as

she put a bowl of grapes and a plate of chocolate chip cookies on the table. "He is crazy about that dog. All he wanted to do all day was follow her around and do everything she did. He even tried to drink from her water bowl!"

Charles looked down at the Bean and shook his head. Who else had a little brother who thought he was a dog? "So we're not keeping Goldie?" he asked.

"Well, we aren't keeping Goldie for good," said his mom, smiling. "But she's sweet to the Bean, so she can stay for a little while. Just until we find her a really good home." Their mom patted Goldie on the head. "She deserves the best."

"Mom!" Lizzie threw her arms around her mother.

Charles couldn't believe his ears. "Really? Really? Goldie is staying with us?"

"Only for a while," his mother answered. "Don't forget that part." She looked down at the Bean. He was tugging at one of her shoelaces while

Goldie tugged at the other. "It's great for the Bean to have such a good friend. But this family is not ready to have a full-time dog. Not yet."

Charles nodded. "Right," he said. He was sure he could convince his mother to keep Goldie forever. He slid down off his chair and sat on the floor next to Goldie. She trotted right over, climbed up into his lap, and started chewing on his ear. It tickled! Charles laughed and kissed the top of the puppy's silky head.

Goldie liked that. This boy made her feel happy and safe. She was so glad to see him again. It seemed like forever *since he had gone away.*

Goldie wagged her little tail as hard as she could as she nibbled and licked and nuzzled. By now, Lizzie had joined Charles on the floor. "Let me hold her for a minute," she said. "Here, Goldie!"

Happily, Goldie climbed over to explore Lizzie's ears. The girl was also wonderful. She smelled good and tasted even better.

Then the Bean started to nibble on Charles's

ears. "Hey!" said Charles. "Mom, tell him he's not a dog!"

"I've been trying to tell him that all day!" his mom said, laughing. Then she sat down at the table and got serious. "So here's the deal," she said. "You two are going to be responsible for this puppy whenever you are home. That means you walk her, you feed her, you make sure she has water. And don't forget our goal: We need to make sure Goldie goes to the best possible home." She looked at Charles, then at Lizzie. "If you do a really good job fostering Goldie, I might start to believe that this family will be ready for a puppy of our own sometime soon."

Charles and Lizzie were nodding eagerly. "Okay, Mom," said Charles.

"We'll start training her right away," promised Lizzie. "It will be easier to find a good home for a puppy that behaves."

"Oh, and one more thing," Mom added. "You also have to take care of all your regular chores. I don't want your rooms to become disaster areas just because we have a puppy in the house." She looked at Charles when she said that. Lizzie was tidy, but Charles's room was usually a mess. "No falling behind on school work." This time she looked at Lizzie, who sometimes waited to do her homework until the last minute.

"No problem," said Charles, even though he hated cleaning his room.

"Absolutely, Mom," promised Lizzie. She held Goldie up and rubbed noses with the pup. "We'll do anything to keep you around, right, sweetie?"

Goldie stuck out her tongue and licked Lizzie's nose. Then she clambered down and started to sniff the floor.

Lizzie jumped up. "That means she has to pee!" she said. "When she sniffs like that we have to get her outside right away. Then we praise her for doing it outside."

Charles scooped up Goldie and ran for the back door. As soon as he got outside, he put her down and watched proudly as she ran straight onto the lawn and squatted. "Good girl!" he said. "You're such a good girl."

Goldie didn't know why the boy was so happy, but it made her happy, too. She ran to him and when he picked her up she licked his face all over.

Charles and Lizzie spent the rest of the afternoon in Lizzie's room. Lizzie had her computer on and all her dog books out. While Charles rolled around on the floor with Goldie, Lizzie told him all about puppy training.

"The most important things for a puppy to learn are" — she held up three fingers — "where to do your business, how to get along with other dogs and with people, and what your name is." She put one finger down for each thing. "Goldie already knows her name, don't you, Goldie?"

Goldie stopped chewing on Charles's foot just long enough to look up. Her eyes were bright and her ears were pricked up.

34

"Good girl!" Lizzie smiled at her. "So we just have to work on the first two: housebreaking and socializing. *Socializing* is the word dog trainers use for 'making friends,'" Lizzie explained to Charles. "Goldie's already learning how to go to the bathroom outdoors. And she gets along well with people. Pretty soon we should start having her meet other dogs," Lizzie went on. "Her mom and her brothers and sisters taught her a little bit about doggy manners, but she'll need more practice."

Charles knew Lizzie was probably right, but he was having too much fun just playing with Goldie to think about training her. At the moment, they were playing a game where she pretended his foot was a big scary monster. He kept it very still while she bravely crept up on it. Then, just as she was about to pounce, he wiggled his foot and Goldie tumbled backward. The next time she crept up, he let her pounce and get the monster. She growled tiny puppy growls as she wrestled with his sock, trying to pull it off of his foot.

After a few rounds, Goldie stopped suddenly, wandered over to the soft rug next to Lizzie's bed, curled up, and fell asleep.

For a while, Charles and Lizzie just stared at her. She was so cute, with one paw over her nose.

"Okay, next," Lizzie said. "We have to convince Mom that we're serious about finding Goldie a great home."

"But I want *this* to be her home," Charles complained.

Lizzie sighed. "Me, too," she said. "But for now we're just her foster home, and that means it's our job to find her the best forever family."

Charles sighed. "We could make a sign," he suggested.

Lizzie was great at using her computer to make signs and birthday cards. She got right to work. "How does this look?" she asked, a few minutes later. She showed Charles a sign decorated with a picture of a golden retriever.

PERFECT PUPPY NEEDS GOOD HOME, it read. The Petersons' phone number was on the bottom.

"It looks good," said Charles. "Maybe *too* good. We don't really want someone to take her away, do we?" He was still wishing they could keep Goldie forever.

"Charles," Lizzie said, "I really don't think Mom is ready for a full-time dog. But if we do a good job with Goldie, it'll show her how responsible we can be." She looked at her sign again. "Still, we don't want to give Goldie up *too* soon." She took out the word PERFECT. "Better?" she asked. When Charles nodded, she printed out ten copies.

"Charles! Lizzie!" called their mother from downstairs. "Time to set the table for dinner!"

They took one of the signs to show their mom and left the others in a pile near Lizzie's backpack, by the door.

"Let's let Goldie sleep," Charles suggested. "She's had a busy day."

They tiptoed out of the room and down the stairs.

Goldie woke up a few minutes later. She stretched and yawned and looked around for her people. Where were they? They had gone away and left her all alone. This was her chance to sniff and explore this fun new place. Goldie roamed all over Lizzie's room, discovering exciting new smells and tastes in every corner.

Finally, Goldie wandered over to the door. There was a pile of scritchy, scratchy fresh new papers. Goldie had been wishing for something to chew and tear apart. These papers looked just right! She dove into the pile and got to work.

CHAPTER SIX

"So, when we went back upstairs after setting the table, there was Goldie, sitting in the middle of a huge pile of shredded paper!" Charles laughed, remembering the "what did I do?" look on Goldie's face when he and Lizzie came into the room. Goldie had destroyed every single one of the signs they had made! But it didn't feel right to yell at her, and Lizzie said there was no point in punishing her after the fact.

Charles was telling the story during Sharing Circle time at school the next morning. Usually he told riddles or knock-knock jokes, but this story was too good to keep to himself. Everybody was laughing. Mr. Mason laughed the loudest.

"That's why my mom borrowed a crate from her friend," Charles went on.

"You mean, like a cage?" asked Merry. "That's horrible. She's a puppy, not an animal in the zoo."

Charles shook his head. "A crate is different from a cage. It's a place where Goldie can feel safe, like a little cave. And it's more fair to her this way. She won't have the chance to destroy things when we're not there to watch her, and we won't have to get mad or punish her." Charles was trying to remember all the things Lizzie had told him about using a crate to train a puppy. He didn't tell Merry that he'd thought the same thing — that it looked like a cage — when he first saw it. But when he saw Goldie walk in on her own and snuggle into the blankets they'd put inside, he understood. Plus, it would help with housebreaking, since puppies don't like to make a mess in the same place where they sleep.

But Charles didn't really want to bring that part up at Sharing Circle. Ben would just make a joke about puppy poo, and everybody would start giggling.

"Goldie is really smart," Charles went on. He knew he was using up more than his fair share of time, but he couldn't help it. "She knows her name, and she knows to come when you call her."

"What if her new family gives her a new name?" Brianna asked.

Charles frowned. He did not want to think about Goldie going to a new family. Lizzie had printed up another batch of signs, and he and his dad had gone out after supper to put some up around town. But Charles hoped that nobody would notice them.

"I have a feeling that Goldie's name suits her perfectly," said Mr. Mason. "I think she'll keep it."

Charles smiled again. "It *is* the perfect name," he said. "Once we got her cleaned up from the fire, her coat really was golden."

Charles looked up at the clock. It was only nine-thirty. How was he going to stand waiting until two-thirty to see Goldie again? He wished he could be hugging her right that minute.

"Goldie sounds like a terrific pup, Charles," said Mr. Mason. "Thanks for telling us about her. Does anybody else have something to share? Sammy, what about you?"

Sammy was looking down at his hands. "Nope," he said.

That was strange. Sammy *always* had something to share. Even if it was totally made up, like the time he told about purple space aliens landing in his backyard.

"How's your dog — his name is Rufus, right?" Mr. Mason asked.

Sammy nodded. And suddenly, Charles knew why Sammy was sad. Hearing about Goldie probably made Sammy feel even worse about Rufus getting so old and slow and boring.

"Has Rufus met Goldie yet?" Mr. Mason asked. Sammy shook his head.

And then Charles had a great idea. "Hey!" he said, even though it wasn't his turn to talk. "Goldie needs to meet other dogs. It's called sho — shoshal —"

"Socialization?" guessed Mr. Mason.

"That's it!" Charles was excited. "It means that it's good for her to make friends."

At recess, Charles and Sammy made plans for Goldie and Rufus to play after school.

By the end of the day, Sammy seemed excited, too. As soon as they got home from school, Charles and Lizzie brought Goldie to the little fenced-in park on the corner. Sammy met them there with Rufus.

"We have to let them start slowly," Lizzie said. She had been reading all about socializing dogs. They were meeting at the park instead of in one of their yards. Lizzie's book said it was important for the first meeting to happen in a place where neither dog was in charge.

"Hey, Rufus," Charles said. "How's the big guy?" Rufus wagged his tail when he saw Charles. He didn't seem to notice the new puppy.

Charles was holding Goldie in his arms. She struggled to get down. "Do you think Rufus is ready?" he asked Sammy.

Sammy had Rufus on a leash, and Rufus sat down next to him. "Sure," said Sammy. "Let's see what happens when you put her down."

"Keep them both on their leashes," Lizzie said as Charles put Goldie on the ground. "Now let Rufus come over and sniff Goldie."

"He probably won't even get up," Sammy started to say. Just then, Rufus jumped to his feet and pulled Sammy off balance. "Hey!"

Rufus was heading straight toward Goldie. But the little pup didn't seem at all scared. She pulled Charles off balance, too.

The two dogs charged for each other.

"Uh-oh," said Sammy. "Dog fight!"

But the dogs did not fight.

They played.

Goldie bowed down with her front paws stretched out. She looked up at Rufus with an expression that said, "Chase me!" And Rufus did. When Goldie dashed off toward the swings, Rufus dashed after her, dragging the leash that Sammy had dropped behind him. When he caught her, they tussled for a few moments. Goldie bit at the big dog's legs while Rufus batted at the puppy's head with a soft paw. Then Goldie took off running, and Rufus chased her around the seesaws.

Goldie loved playing with Rufus. She ran and rolled and tumbled. What a happy day! What a great new friend!

"Look at Rufus go!" shouted Sammy with a laugh. "That's the most running he's done in a month."

"He sure looks happy," Charles agreed. Charles looked at Sammy and thought that he looked happy, too.

"It's all about the socialization," Lizzie said smugly.

They all laughed as Rufus rolled over and let Goldie pounce on his belly.

Just then, Dad came jogging down the street. "Charles! Lizzie!" he called. "You need to bring Goldie home. Some people saw our sign. They might want to adopt her, and they're coming over right now!"

CHAPTER SEVEN

Charles and Lizzie stared at their father. "What?" Charles asked.

"Somebody already called?" Lizzie said at the same time.

"Dad!" Charles wailed. Just then, Rufus chased Goldie right into Charles. "Oof," he said, bending down to pick Goldie up. He held her tight. "Nobody's taking you," he whispered into her ear. "It's too soon."

"Charles, I know your mom talked to you about this. We agreed that we'd keep Goldie — but only until we found her a good home." His dad reached out to pat Goldie's head. "Who's a good girl?" he said softly.

Charles could tell his dad didn't want Goldie to go, either.

"But how do we *know* if it's a good home?" Charles asked.

"We interview them, that's how," said Lizzie. "I already did some research on this. I downloaded a questionnaire we can use."

Dad looked a little surprised. "Well — that's interesting, Lizzie, but really, I'm not sure it's necessary. These people sound very nice, and —"

"Do they have a fenced-in yard?" Lizzie demanded. "Do they understand the nutritional needs of a puppy? Is someone going to be home most of the day?"

Now Dad *really* looked surprised. "You know," he said, "those are actually very good questions. I suppose it couldn't hurt to ask some of them."

Charles still couldn't believe they were going to have to give up Goldie. "But, Dad," he said. "Can't we keep her? Please?"

Dad shook his head. "A full-time dog is a lot of

responsibility," he said. "Now, if we were talking about a *cat*," he said, "your mom might feel differently."

Charles knew Dad was trying to make him smile, but he just couldn't.

"Okay," said Dad. "Look, we have to get home. They'll be here any minute." He glanced over at Rufus, who stood panting next to Sammy. Rufus's eyes were bright as he stared up at Goldie. His tongue was hanging out as he panted happily. He obviously wanted to play some more. "Is that the dog you were telling us about yesterday?" Dad asked Sammy. "He sure doesn't *look* bored and lazy. Exhausted, maybe, but not bored."

As he picked up the leash, Sammy smiled at Rufus. "I know," he said. "He's like a whole other dog. He liked playing with Goldie." Rufus licked Sammy's hand.

"I bet your dad will be happy. I know he misses his old sidekick. I used to see them out running together early in the morning." Dad started walking back toward home. "Come on, guys," he said. "We need to get Goldie home, so she can meet these folks who want to adopt her."

Mom was mopping the kitchen floor when they walked in. "Hey!" she said. "Watch the footprints. I don't want these people to think we're slobs."

"Mom," Lizzie said, "it doesn't matter what *they* think of *us*."

"I know," her mom said. "But they sound like a sweet older couple. They want to take Goldie with them in their RV when they head down to Florida this winter."

"Older couple?" Lizzie asked doubtfully.

"RV?" Charles asked. He knew what that was. A tiny little house on wheels. Not a place for a young golden retriever.

"Goldie needs a home where she can run around," Lizzie said. "She's going to need a lot of exercise. Look at her! She's been playing around for an hour, and she's not even tired."

It was true. At that moment, Goldie was

bounding after the Bean. He had her Duckie and he was toddling away as fast as he could. Goldie grabbed hold of one of the wings and the Bean sat down with a *bump*.

Everybody waited for a second. Was he going to start crying?

But the Bean just laughed his googly laugh.

Just then, the doorbell rang. Nobody ever used the front door, much less the doorbell.

"That must be them!" said Mom, wiping her hands on a towel.

"I'll get the interview forms," Lizzie said. She dashed upstairs.

Charles followed his parents to the door. The Bean and Goldie followed Charles.

There was a long, boring round of introductions as the people — a tiny gray-haired lady and a tall, stoop-shouldered bald man — came in and sat down in the living room.

"We are so excited about having a little puppy to keep us company," the woman said.

"Well, here she is," said Mom. "This is Goldie." She picked up Goldie and brought her over to put her in the lady's lap.

"Why, isn't she adorable?" said the lady. But Charles noticed that she set Goldie back down on the floor without even kissing her once.

"Hey there, little champ," said the man, bending down to give Goldie a hearty pat on the ribs. "Aren't you a sturdy little thing?"

Goldie wondered who these people were. Why were they here? Her people were being nice to these new folks, so Goldie tried to be nice, too. She put her paws up on the man's knees and barked happily.

"Goldie!" said Mom. "She doesn't usually do that," she told the people. "She's really very well behaved."

Charles stared at his mother. Was she really thinking of giving Goldie to these people?

Lizzie pounded down the stairs with some papers in her hand. "Got it!" she said. She plopped down in a chair. "Do you have a bed prepared for Goldie?" she asked, without waiting for an introduction.

"Lizzie," Dad began, "this is Mr. —"

But she rushed right along. "Is your house puppy-proofed? Which of you will be the primary caretaker? Have you looked into a puppy kindergarten class? Which vet will you take Goldie to?"

Lizzie wasn't even waiting for answers.

Not that it mattered. Charles could see that the man and the lady were obviously not about to answer. The lady looked from Lizzie to her husband. "Well, I never!" she grumbled, and the man just sat there with his arms crossed and his eyebrows raised.

"I'm sorry," said Mom. "Please don't mind my daughter. You seem like very nice people, and I'm sure —"

Just then, Goldie took the cuff of the man's pants in her teeth and started to pull, growling a little as she shook it back and forth. Suddenly, there was a loud ripping noise. A surprised Goldie sat back hard, holding a shred of material in her mouth.

The man's eyes grew wide.

His wife stopped grumbling.

And Charles burst out laughing.

CHAPTER EIGHT

Charles put his hand over his mouth and tried to stop laughing, but he couldn't. The look on the man's face! The look on *Goldie's* face! It was too much.

He thought he saw the corners of his father's mouth twitching. Lizzie was obviously holding back a giggle. And even his mom seemed to have a tiny sparkle in her eyes. "Oh, dear," said Mom. "I'm so sorry!"

"Puppies will be puppies," said Dad. He shook his head, laughing a little.

"Well!" The woman stood up. "Come on, Harold. We'll have to look elsewhere for a dog we can live with. A dog with some *manners*."

She walked past the Bean, who was crawling on the floor near Goldie. The Bean looked up at her and barked. The woman jumped — and kept on walking, a little more quickly.

Goldie watched as the two strangers walked out of the room. The piece of cloth dropped out of her mouth as she watched them go. Why were they going away? Then Charles sat down on the floor next to her and invited her into his lap, and she forgot all about the strangers.

When they heard the front door close, the whole family burst out laughing. "A dog with some manners!" Dad gasped. "What would it say? Please pass the dog food?"

"May I please go for a walk?" Lizzie added.

"Thank you for the lovely bath!" Charles shouted.

"Maybe what they really need is a cat," suggested Mom.

They laughed for a long time.

Then Mom got serious. "Oh, dear," she said.

"What if we just drove away the perfect family for Goldie?"

"Come on, Mom," said Lizzie. "They weren't the right people for Goldie. Can you imagine her cooped up in an RV?"

"I guess not," Mom admitted. "But we really have to find this dog a home before she destroys our entire house."

Charles gave Goldie a little squeeze and she let out a tiny sigh. He could hardly stand the idea of giving her up. But if they really couldn't keep her, she deserved the best home, with people who loved her just the way she was.

"She's probably ready for a trip outside," Lizzie suggested. "Let's take her out back."

Sammy must have been watching from next door. He came right over. "So?" he asked. "Didn't those people want her?"

Charles shook his head. "She didn't give them the best first impression," he said. He told Sammy what had happened.

"Well, it doesn't matter," Sammy said. "Because I thought of a great home for Goldie."

"What?" Charles asked. "Where?"

Sammy pointed to his house, next door. "Right there," he said. "She could live with me and Rufus. Come on, it's perfect! She's just what Rufus needs. Didn't you see how happy he was, playing with her?"

Goldie living next door with Sammy? Charles wasn't sure how he felt about that. What if Goldie ended up liking Sammy better?

"What, really?" Lizzie asked. "Your parents said it was okay?" She didn't seem so sure about the idea, either.

"Well, no," Sammy said. "Actually — I haven't asked them yet." He looked a little sheepish. "But they *have* to say yes."

Charles thought some more. It was true that Goldie was good for Rufus. And if she lived next door, he could see her every day. Suddenly, it seemed like a *great* idea. "If we can't keep Goldie, having her next door would be the next best thing," he said.

Lizzie looked at him. "You know," she said slowly, "you might be right."

"He's *definitely* right," Sammy said. "Now all we have to do is convince my parents."

"We can do it," Charles said. "Goldie is the best puppy ever. How could they say no?"

Sammy and Charles and Lizzie brought Goldie right over to meet Sammy's parents. Charles held her in his arms so she wouldn't get down and chase around with Rufus, breaking things and making a mess. Sammy's dad said that Goldie looked like a great pup. "But we already *have* a dog," he added. "And I'm not sure I can go through the whole housebreaking thing again. Rufus took *months* to learn. What a disaster! It was too much work."

Sammy's mother thought Goldie was very cute. "But it's been hard on us, watching Rufus get older. I don't think we want to start all over. We don't really need another dog now." She smiled at Lizzie and Charles. "I'm sure you'll have no trouble finding a good home for her," she said.

Charles knew she was right. But if he really had to give up Goldie, the *best* home would be one that was right next door to his own!

"If only she was housebroken," Sammy said when they were back outside. "Maybe that would convince Dad."

"Sure, as long as she didn't decide to chew his favorite camera or something," Lizzie said. Sammy's dad was a photographer, and he had a lot of expensive equipment.

They both sounded as if they had given up. But Charles wasn't ready to quit. He wanted Goldie to live next door! "It's time for Operation Goldie," he declared. "They might not *need* another dog, but we can make them *want* another dog. Goldie's so smart. She just has to learn a few things, and then Sammy's parents won't be able to resist her."

Lizzie and Sammy stared at him.

"That's true!" Lizzie said. "We can train her so they don't have to."

"I bet we can teach her to always go outside," Sammy said. "She only makes mistakes once in a while."

"And puppies need to chew," Lizzie said. "That's a fact. But we can make sure she has her own toys to chew on, so she won't wreck people's things."

Cozy in Charles's arms, Goldie looked happily from one face to another. Her people were excited. Something good was going to happen. She could hardly wait!

CHAPTER NINE

"Come, Goldie!" Lizzie knelt down with her arms wide open. Goldie dashed across the yard so fast that she tumbled head over heels twice before she got to Lizzie. "Oh, what a good girl," Lizzie said.

"Come, Goldie!" called Charles from another corner of the yard, and Goldie took off at a gallop. Charles was proud of Goldie for learning so fast.

"Look at her go!" Sammy said. He looked at the list in his hand. "I think we can check off 'comes when called,'" he said. "She sure knows how to do that."

"And 'sit,' and even 'stay,'" added Lizzie. "She's got those nailed."

Charles kissed the top of Goldie's head as he

cuddled the wriggling pup in his arms. Operation Goldie was a total success so far. Lizzie said they could only train Goldie for ten minutes at a time because of her short attention span. But she had learned so much in one week! She really was the smartest puppy ever. And Charles had been watching Sammy with Goldie. His friend was great with the puppy.

Maybe the plan would really work, and Sammy's parents would agree to keep her! Charles would get to play with her every day and watch her grow up. He could already see himself and Sammy throwing balls for Rufus and a grown-up Goldie, taking the dogs swimming at Loon Lake, showing them off at the library's annual pet show.

"And it's been" — Sammy checked the sheet again — "three whole days since she made a mistake in the house."

"Two days," Lizzie reminded him. "Remember that little incident in the entryway?"

"That doesn't count!" Charles said. "She was

trying to get outside!" He knelt down to give Goldie a rub. "Weren't you, girl?" he asked.

"The chewing has gotten a lot better, too," Lizzie said. "The only thing she's destroyed lately is Duckie, and that was okay, since he's a dog toy."

"She destroyed Duckie?" Sammy asked. He looked upset.

"Well, not really *destroyed,*" Charles said. "Let's just say that he's a lot thinner than he used to be. And he probably won't be flying south for the winter."

Sammy laughed. He reached down to pat Goldie. "That's okay, Goldie. Rufus was tired of that old toy, anyway."

"I think Goldie will be ready to show off to your parents in just a few more days," Lizzie said.

"Charles! Lizzie!" Their mom was standing at the back door. "Guess what? We just got another phone call. A family is interested in adopting Goldie!"

Charles, Lizzie, and Sammy stared at one another. This was terrible news! Nobody else could adopt Goldie. Not now, not when they had worked so hard with her.

"Come on in, I'll tell you all about it," said Mom.

Lizzie, Charles, and Sammy all went inside.

The news got worse and worse. According to Mom, this family sounded great. They weren't old people living in an RV. They had three kids, and they lived in the country, where Goldie would have lots of room to roam. And they were coming right over to see Goldie. They would be there in half an hour!

When their mom left the kitchen after telling them about the phone call, Lizzie and Charles and Sammy just sat there. They stared down at Goldie. "I guess that's it," Sammy said sadly. "We'll never see her again."

"I can't stand it," Lizzie said, getting down on the floor to cuddle with Goldie.

"Hold on, you guys," Charles said. "We can't give up yet."

"What other choice do we have?" Sammy asked.

"We show her off to your parents — *now*," Charles said. "Sure, we wanted to train her for another few days, but she's nearly perfect. I bet they'll love her."

Lizzie and Sammy and Charles looked at one another.

Yes. It was time.

Lizzie started getting all bossy and making plans. "Okay," she said. "Let me see that checklist. We need to figure out all the things we want to show off. First we'll have her sit. Then we'll show how well she can stay —"

Goldie could tell that something exciting was about to happen, but until it did, she decided she might as well have a drink! She was so thirsty. She wandered over to her bowl and drank some water. Then she waded into her water bowl a little

66

bit, because she liked how the cool water felt on her feet. This was fun! She had another drink. Then, suddenly, Charles came over and picked her up.

"Ready to show off your stuff, Goldie?" he asked. "This is the big time. You have to do your very, very best."

Goldie licked his face. Charles laughed and gave her a kiss on the nose. "Let's go, girl," he said.

When they got to Sammy's house, Sammy put Rufus in the downstairs den and shut the door. They had agreed that Goldie would be more impressive if she wasn't distracted. Then he called his parents into the living room. "I know you think a puppy is too much bother," he said, "but this one is different. She's perfectly trained! She won't be any trouble at all."

"Sammy —" his dad began.

"Please, Dad?" Sammy begged. "Can we just show you all the things Goldie can do?"

Sammy's mom and dad looked at each other. "Okay," said his dad, leaning back on the couch. "Let's see this perfect dog perform."

Lizzie was first. "Here, Goldie," she called, and Goldie came trotting right over to her. "Goldie, sit!" Lizzie said.

Goldie sat.

Sammy's mom clapped her hands. "Excellent!" she cheered.

Next Sammy called Goldie. When she came, he praised her. Then he said, "Goldie, down!"

Goldie lay down, her eyes on Sammy's face.

That made Charles feel a little jealous. But he was also proud of Goldie.

"Wow," said Sammy's dad. "That really is pretty good."

Then Charles called Goldie. "Goldie, here!" he said, with a big smile. He had a good feeling about the way this was going.

Goldie started to run over to Charles. But

on her way, she stopped on a pretty rug under the piano.

She sniffed.

She squatted.

And she peed.

CHAPTER TEN

Sammy's father groaned.

His mother sighed.

"This is exactly what I'm talking about," said Sammy's father.

"But, Dad!" Sammy said. "She really is house-broken! I don't know what happened."

"What happened is that she's a puppy," his dad said tiredly. "Puppies make mistakes. It's not her fault. But this is just the kind of thing that I don't want to deal with."

Lizzie picked Goldie up and took her outside.

Sammy's mom ran to the kitchen and came back with some paper towels.

Charles just sat there, feeling awful.

They had tried so hard! Goldie had tried so

hard! And now everything was ruined. Instead of living right next door, Goldie was going to live far away with some perfect family in their perfect country home. He would never see her again, never feel her sweet puppy breath on his face, never get another puppy hug from her little paws, never see her grow up into a happy, healthy dog.

Sammy's father was shaking his head. "We went through it all with Rufus," he said. "Remember our wedding?" he asked Sammy's mom.

She thought for a second and laughed.

"What's so funny?" Sammy asked.

"Rufus was in our wedding," his mom explained. "He was our ring bearer. Our wedding rings were tied to his collar with white ribbon, and he was supposed to sit there quietly until the moment came when the minister said we should exchange rings." She started to laugh. "Instead, he tore up and down the aisle of the church, barking and chasing his tail and chewing the maid of honor's bouquet."

"And then, right in front of everybody, he peed

on my shoe!" Sammy's dad added. He was laughing so hard that Charles could hardly understand him. "What a moment!" He shook his head. Then he stopped laughing and a sad look came into his eyes. "Good old Rufus," he said. "He used to be quite a dog." Sammy's father reached out to hold hands with Sammy's mom.

Suddenly, Charles had an idea. Rufus was *still* quite a dog — when he was with Goldie! So far, Sammy's parents had not seen the two of them together. That's why Sammy's family needed Goldie — for Rufus.

Charles looked over at Sammy.

"Get Rufus!" he whispered.

Sammy raised his eyebrows. "Why?" he whispered back.

"Just get him."

Suddenly, Sammy nodded. He understood. He jumped to his feet and ran for the den. A second later, Rufus plodded into the living room. By then, Lizzie had returned with Goldie.

When Rufus saw Goldie, his eyes brightened and his ears went up. His tail started wagging. He woofed a little woof and bowed down with his front paws way out in front.

Goldie was overjoyed. Her friend! What a great surprise! It had been so long since she had seen him. Oh, happy, happy, happy.

Goldie bounced out of Lizzie's arms and touched noses with Rufus. Then she gave him a look that said, "Chase me!" She took off, zooming around the coffee table and running behind the couch.

Rufus took off after her, woofing happily as he skidded past Sammy's parents. "Whoa!" said Sammy's father.

"I haven't seen him look that happy in months," said Sammy's mother.

Sammy's dad watched Rufus let Goldie chase him into the front hallway. "He's acting like a puppy," he said wonderingly.

"He always does when Goldie's around," Sammy

said. "That's why we think she should come and live with us."

Sammy's parents didn't say anything for a few minutes. They just laughed and pointed as Rufus and Goldie wrestled on the floor by their feet.

"So?" Charles finally asked. "What do you think?"

"I think," said Sammy's father, "that if Goldie makes Rufus this happy, maybe a few puddles here and there would be a small price to pay. It's good to see the old guy playing again."

"Does that mean —" Charles could hardly believe it.

Sammy's mom looked at Sammy's dad. Then she nodded. "I think it means you found a new home for Goldie," she said. "She's going to be your neighbor."

That night, the Petersons celebrated with pizza. Pepperoni for Charles, olives for Lizzie, and extra cheese for the Bean. It was great to know Goldie would be living right next door.

"I have to admit that you kids really did a great job with Goldie," Mom said. "Plus, you kept your side of the deal. Lizzie, you kept up with your homework. And Charles, your room is cleaner than I've ever seen it. I'm proud of you both."

"So does that mean we get our own puppy soon?" Charles asked.

"We'll see," said Mom. "It does seem awfully quiet around here without a puppy in the house."

Charles wasn't sure whether she thought that was a good or a bad thing. He decided not to push it. "I felt sorry for that family with the three kids," he said. "They really wanted a dog, too."

"But Goldie went to the right home," Lizzie said. "Did you see how happy Sammy's parents looked? And Rufus is like a whole new dog."

"Plus," said Charles, around a mouthful of pizza, "we get to see Goldie every day."

"Woof!" said the Bean, from his spot on the floor next to Charles.

"Maybe we could foster another puppy someday," Charles suggested, "even if we're not ready for a dog of our own."

"Hmm," said Dad. "Not a bad idea."

"It's a *great* idea," said Lizzie.

"Woof!" agreed the Bean.

Even Mom was nodding. "Well, I guess we do have some leftover puppy food. I'd hate to see that go to waste."

Charles imagined puppies of every size and breed, from giant Great Danes to teeny tiny Chihuauas. He wondered what kind of puppy the Petersons would foster next. But he knew it really didn't matter. All puppies were wonderful. Whatever kind the next one was, he would love it and take care of it and find it the very best home. And maybe someday, if he was lucky, that home would be his own.

PUPPY TIPS

Puppy Buddies

Lizzie and Charles had the right idea when they decided to *socialize* Goldie. Every dog should learn to be comfortable with people and other dogs. Plus, what could be more fun than watching your best friend play with his or her buddies?

But when puppies are very young, they should only play with dogs you know. A puppy that hasn't had its final puppy shots (this usually happens when the puppy is 12 weeks old) could get sick if it plays with a dog that hasn't had all of its shots. And unless you know the dog and its owner, you can't be sure that a dog is healthy. Charles and Lizzie knew that Sammy's family takes great care of Rufus, so they knew it was safe for Goldie to play with him.

Ask your vet for more information about this— or any other questions you might have about raising a puppy.

Dear Reader,

I love puppies! I got my black Labrador retriever, Django, when he was a puppy. (The "D" in his name is silent, so you say it "Jango.")

I remember Django's puppy days very well, even though he is now nine years old. He had ten brothers and sisters! He was a good puppy. (Well, he did pee in the house a few times.) And he grew up to be a very good dog. Django loves to eat, swim, fetch, and get patted. We have a lot of fun.

Do you have a puppy or a dog? What kind? If you don't have a puppy, what kind would you like to have?

Yours from the Puppy Place,
Ellen Miles